Can You Find It?

T0060925

Let's Celebrate!

A Can-You-Find-It Book

by Sarah L. Schuette

PEBBLE
a capstone imprint

Seasons

Can you find these things?

guitar

cat

snail

taco

tractor

cherries

skateboard

pie

zebra

wagon

Fiesta!

Can you find these things?

spider

pineapple

avocado

nose

key

llama

pig

hanger

sun

rose

Happy Birthday

Can you find these things?

goldfish

poodle

tennis ball

helicopter

car

rainbow

cell phone

frog

seahorse

piñata

Fireworks

Can you find these things?

milk jug

flute

penguin

hockey skate

astronaut

shovel

skunk

crown

ax

orca

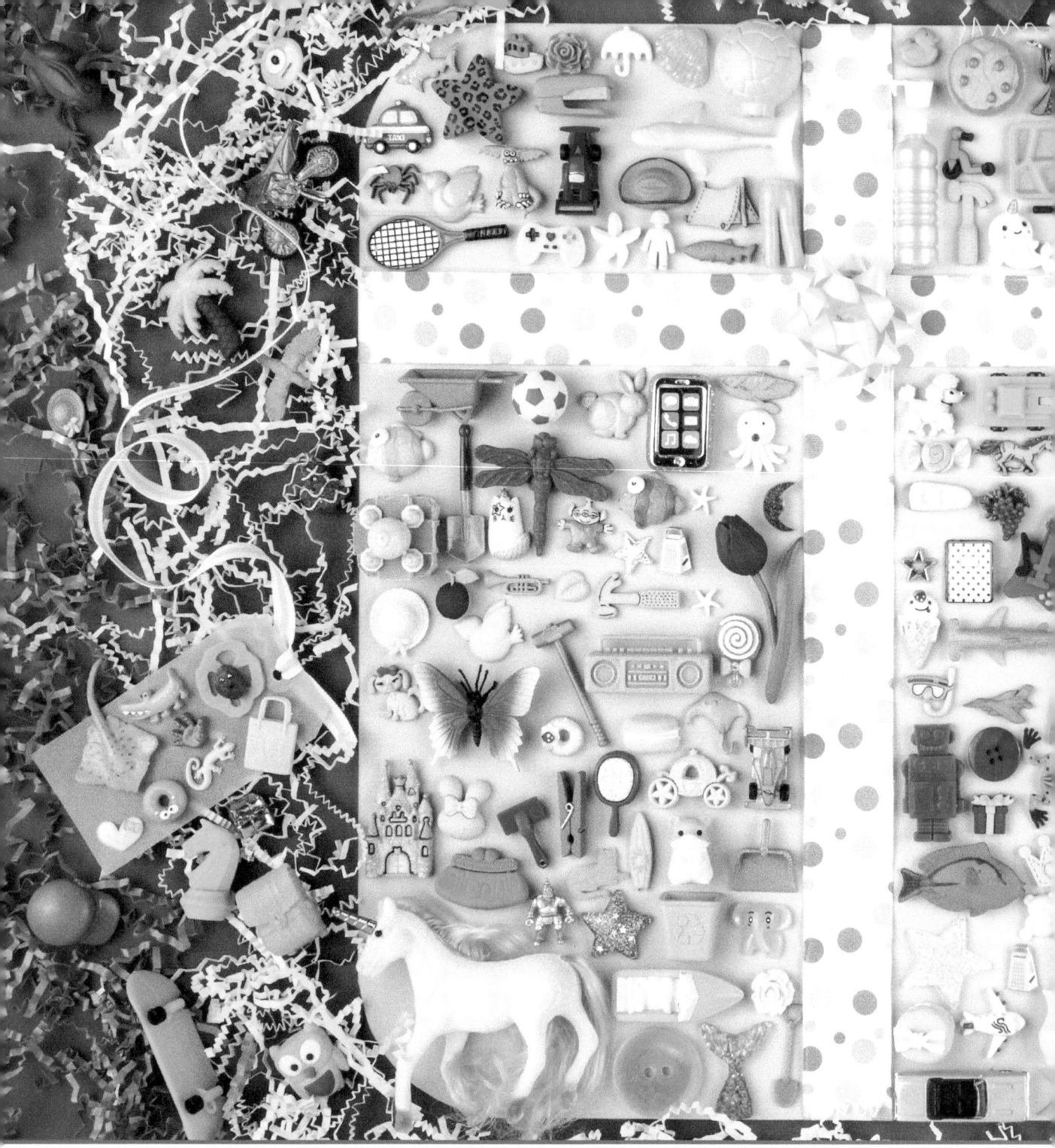

Gift Card

Can you find these things?

caterpillar

Earth

tent

palm tree

cup

owl

surfboard

gift bag

paperclip

eggplant

Love

Can you find these things?

mitten

bird

candle

roller skate

fire truck

crab

chicken

lips

watermelon

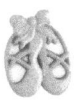

ballet shoes

Holiday Break

Can you find these things?

tape

pickle

moon

trumpet

airplane

hot dog

cactus

strawberry

pear

corncob

Día de los Muertos

Can you find these things?

umbrella

grapes

bicycle

shark

flamingo

hot air balloon

starfish

ice-cream cone

mushroom

pumpkin

Trick or Treat?

Can you find these things?

snowman

basketball

rocking horse

grill

Santa's hat

ping-pong paddle

firefighter

cowboy hat

clamshell

cupcake

Trim the Tree

Can you find these things?

unicorn

heart

pizza

horseshoe

pliers

ghost

flashlight

spoon

snowflake

carrot

Happy New Year!

Can you find these things?

light bulb

camera

cake

clover

drum

stapler

apple

cookies

rake

rat

Earth Day

Can you find these things?

wrench

tissue box

pants

toaster

heart

book

candy cane

cow

star

blender

Lucky Day!

Can you find these things?

mermaid

elephant

anchor

button

puppy

milkshake

ladybug

spatula

sailboat

moose

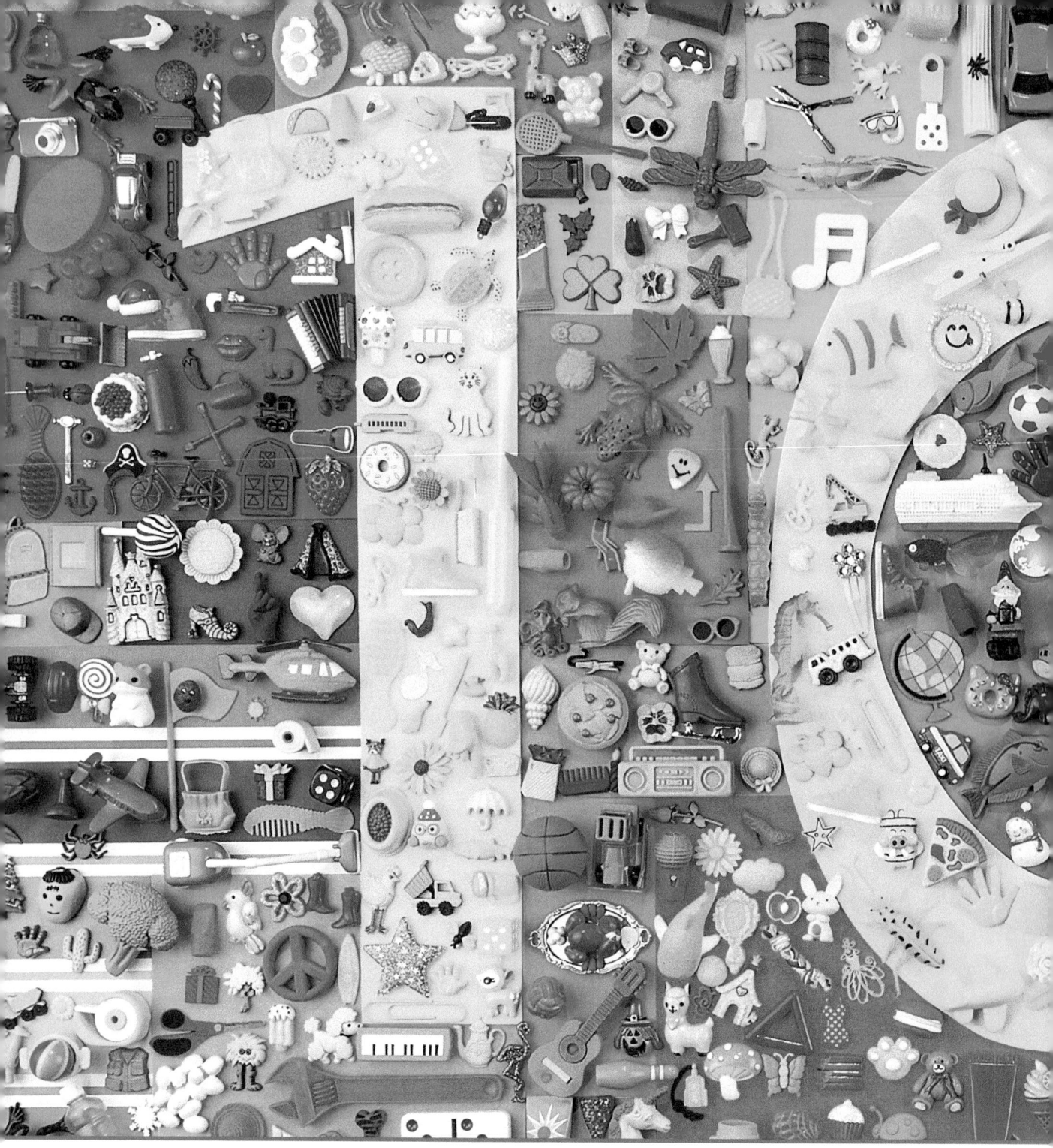

Challenge Puzzle

100th Day of School

Can you find these things?

spray bottle

trophy

bird

knife

red pepper

microphone

caterpillar

toilet paper

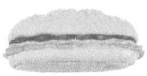

sandwich

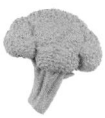

broccoli

Challenge Puzzle: 100th Day of School Answer Key

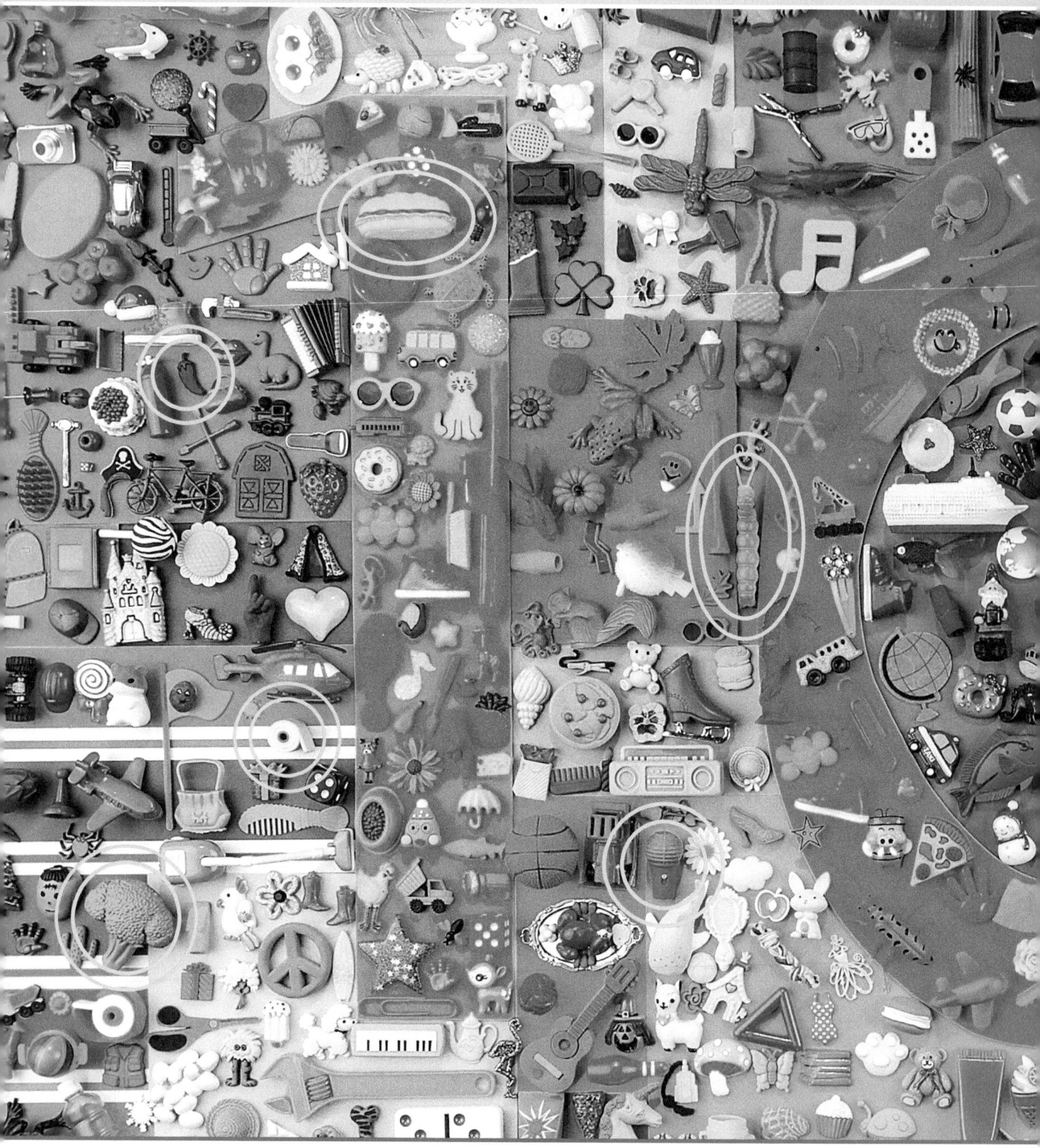

Psst! Did you know that Pebs the Pebble was hiding in EVERY PUZZLE in this book?

It's true! Go back and look!

Look for all the other books in this series:

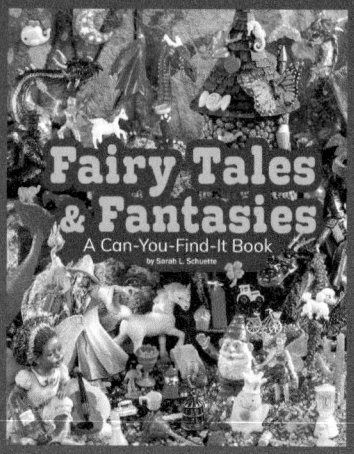

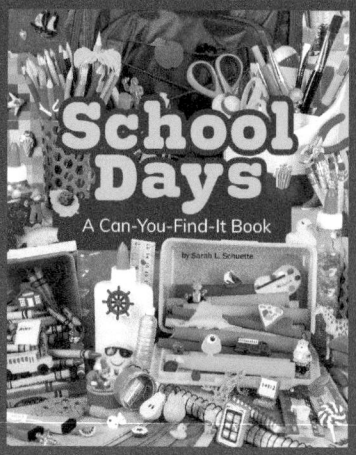

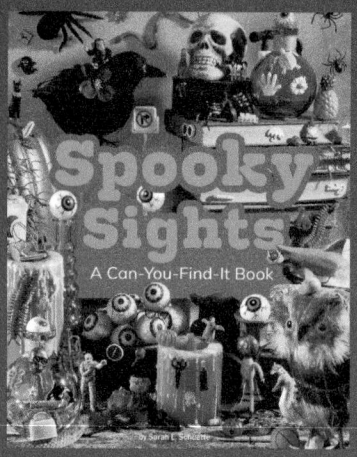

The author dedicates this book to her nieces, Ava and Faith Hahn.

Pebble Sprout is published by Pebble, an imprint of Capstone.
1710 Roe Crest Drive, North Mankato, Minnesota 56003
www.capstonepub.com

Copyright © 2021 by Capstone. All rights reserved. No part of this publication may be reproduced in whole or in part, or stored in a retrieval system, or transmitted in any form or by any means, electronic, mechanical, photocopying, recording, or otherwise, without written permission of the publisher.

Library of Congress Cataloging-in-Publication Data is available on the Library of Congress website.
Names: Schuette, Sarah L., 1976- author.
Title: Let's celebrate! : a can-you-find-it book / by Sarah L. Schuette.
Description: North Mankato : Pebble, 2020. | Series: Can you find it? |
Audience: Ages 4-8 (provided by Pebble) | Description based on print version record and CIP data provided by publisher; resource not viewed.
Identifiers: LCCN 2019057497 (print) | LCCN 2019057498 (ebook)
ISBN 9781977122599 (library binding) | ISBN 9781977126252 (paperback)
ISBN 9781977123114 (eBook PDF)
Subjects: LCSH: Schools—Juvenile literature. | Picture puzzles—Juvenile literature.
Classification: LCC LB1556 (ebook) | LCC LB1556 .S38 2020 (print) |
DDC 793.73—dc23 LC record available at https://lccn.loc.gov/2019057497

Image Credits
All photos by Capstone Studio: Karon Dubke

Editorial Credits
Shelly Lyons, editor; Heidi Thompson, designer; Marcy Morin, set stylist; Morgan Walters, media researcher; Kathy McColley, production specialist

Printed in the United States 6019